About Skill Builders American History: Presidents

by Deborah and Larry Morris

Welcome to Rainbow Bridge Publishing's Skill Builders series. Like our Summer Bridge Activities collection, the Skill Builders series is designed to make learning both fun and rewarding.

Skill Builders American History: Presidents features write-ups on every American president from George Washington to George W. Bush. Pages include basic historical facts, major accomplishments, timelines, fun "do-you-know" facts, and activities to both reinforce comprehension and place the presidents into historical context. A "Days of Youth" section offers added insight into the growing-up years of America's chief executives.

Learning is more effective when approached with an element of fun and enthusiasm—just as most children approach life. That's why the Skill Builders combine entertaining and academically sound exercises with eye-catching graphics and fun themes—to make reviewing basic skills at school or home fun and effective, for both you and your budding scholars.

Table of Contents

George Washington, First of Many

Data & Dates

1732: Born February 22
1775: Chosen to lead Continental Army
1789: Created first official Thanksgiving
1791: Bill of Rights added to Constitution
1794: Put down Whiskey Rebellion
1799: Died December 14 at 67 after riding his horse for hours in bad weather

Details, Details: Washington was married to wealthy widow Martha Dandridge Custis; after their marriage, they lived at Mount Vernon, a family home. He had no children of his own but was stepfather to two. In the first presidential election there were no political parties, and Washington had no opponent; in the second election he was a member of the Federalist party.

Days of Youth: George grew up as the son of a landowner and planter. An older brother helped raise George when their father died. George was educated in reading, writing, and mathematics, but he never attended college. He worked as a surveyor, or mapper of land.

He Did It: As commander of the Continental Army, Washington helped win the Revolutionary War. Six years later Washington was elected president, something he had never wanted. He was a model for future presidents: he chose his own cabinet members and asked their advice, established how the U.S. settles treaties, decided what laws to veto, set traditions for speech making—the inaugural address, the state-of-the-union address, and the farewell address—attended the inaugural address of his successor, and appointed the first federal judges. Political parties formed during his presidency, even though he discouraged it.

Did You Know? Washington is the only man ever unanimously elected president. He had only one tooth of his own—his false teeth were made from elephant and walrus tusks, plus cow, hippo, and human teeth. He was the only president to have a state as well as the nation's capital named after him.

3

George Washington, First of Many

The Whiskey Rebellion: Washington was first in many of the things he accomplished during his two terms. Read about the Whiskey Rebellion, and find seven different words or phrases that can mean "first." Underline them.

To begin with, in 1791, Congress ordered a tax on whiskey. Farmers were initially angry, then outraged. They sold most of their corn at market, but they found that the best way to use their extra corn was to make whiskey. Some people originally used the whiskey as money.

Washington ordered federal officers to collect the whiskey tax. In the beginning, everyone paid the tax. However, the farmers in western Pennsylvania were ready to rebel against the officers from the start. They would not pay the tax. On top of it all, the state's governor refused to punish them.

The rebellion became the nation's highest priority, so Washington formed a volunteer army to enforce the law. When the rebels saw the army with Washington at the front, they turned and fled. Washington put down the Whiskey Rebellion and proved the government could enforce its laws.

4

John Adams, Father of a President

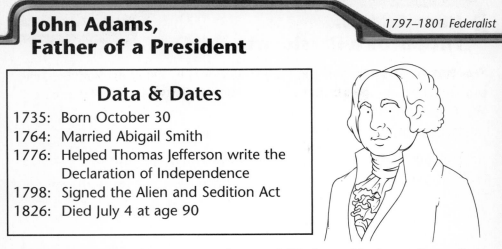

Data & Dates

1735: Born October 30
1764: Married Abigail Smith
1776: Helped Thomas Jefferson write the Declaration of Independence
1798: Signed the Alien and Sedition Act
1826: Died July 4 at age 90

Details, Details: Adams was nicknamed "Father of Independence." He became vice president when he came in second to Washington in the second presidential election. He later became president with only a three-vote lead over Thomas Jefferson; he was the only president to have a vice president from a different political party—Jefferson was a Democratic-Republican. Adams was often gone on government business for long periods of time. He and his wife wrote hundreds of letters to each other during these times.

Days of Youth: John grew up on a farm in Braintree, Massachusetts. As a child he was fond of flying kites, sailing toy boats, and playing a fast game of marbles. He graduated in law from Harvard and practiced law for 12 years.

He Did It: Adams spent most of his presidency avoiding war with France. He appointed hundreds of federal judges, including Chief Justice John Marshall. Many of his appointments, called "Midnight Judges," were named too late in Adams's term to take office.

Did You Know? Adams found being vice president dull and of little value. He was one of only two presidents to sign the Declaration of Independence—the other was Thomas Jefferson. Both men died on the 50th anniversary of the approval of the Declaration. Adams and his wife, Abigail, were the first occupants of the White House. They got lost looking for the White House because it was surrounded by trees. The first lady later hung her laundry in the East Room. It was Adams's idea to celebrate the Fourth of July with fireworks. At age 89 he watched his son, John Quincy Adams, become president.

Presidents 4–5—RB-904000

John Adams, Father of a President

A Letter to Abigail: Find the following words in the word search. Then put the words in the correct space in the letter.

Declaration	Jefferson	France	celebration
Independence	lawyer	Federalist	Quincy
Massachusetts	fireworks	John	president

```
f  m  u  e  k  c  o  n  l  a  w  y  e  r  u
x  a  c  f  e  t  w  y  w  t  v  n  q  k  u
w  s  e  e  e  i  i  t  j  p  h  o  a  r  e
m  s  l  d  f  q  n  q  p  k  l  i  g  c  l
i  a  e  e  o  u  d  f  r  x  a  t  n  v  y
x  c  b  r  s  i  e  s  e  j  z  a  f  i  j
t  h  r  a  j  n  p  k  s  e  r  r  l  k  t
j  u  a  l  o  c  e  r  i  f  u  a  v  l  m
k  s  t  i  h  y  n  o  d  f  x  l  d  w  j
u  e  i  s  n  z  d  w  e  e  k  c  s  w  p
u  t  o  t  g  r  e  e  n  r  p  e  v  v  f
l  t  n  b  k  z  n  r  t  s  n  d  e  p  b
n  s  r  i  g  w  c  i  k  o  d  n  r  h  b
h  z  d  n  c  z  e  f  j  n  p  u  w  r  x
c  r  i  l  y  i  v  z  d  g  h  q  h  m  d
```

June 30, 1799

Dear Abigail,

    When Thomas _____ and I wrote the _____ of _____ so many years ago, we never dreamed that one day I would be _____. I wanted to be a _____ and practice law at home in _____. Now I find that I am continually trying to keep the country out of war with _____. Yet there is so much that gives me hope. Our son _____ _____ is such a good man. I think he will do well in politics. Now we have a great _____ ahead on the Fourth of July. I look forward to seeing you and watching the _____ in the sky.

    Your loving husband,
John

Thomas Jefferson, Man of Many Talents

Data & Dates

1743: Born April 13
1776: Wrote Declaration of Independence
1803: Louisiana Purchase
1807: Signed Embargo Act
1826: Died on July 4 at age 83

Details, Details: Jefferson served as governor of Virginia, a representative to the Continental Congress, U.S. minister to France, secretary of state to George Washington, and vice president to John Adams. In the election of 1800, the electoral college vote was tied; it took 2 months and 36 ballots to declare Jefferson president and his opponent, Aaron Burr, vice president. Jefferson's inauguration was the first time political power in the U.S. passed peacefully from one party to another. He designed his home, Monticello, and designed and organized the University of Virginia.

Days of Youth: From the age of 9, Tom lived with a tutor and was schooled there; he later lost his father at 14. Tom was educated in math, science, philosophy, law, literature, and languages—including French, Greek, and Latin; he grew up to be a lawyer, architect, philosopher, and author.

He Did It: Jefferson stressed unity and toleration. His first crisis involved the Barbary Pirates, who had attacked U.S. ships for years, demanding payments. By 1801, the U.S. had paid almost two million dollars to pirates. Jefferson sent ships to Tripoli, and finally a treaty was signed, but ships from other countries continued to attack for 10 more years. The Louisiana Purchase created a huge irony for Jefferson because a strong central government was now needed to run the massive country—something to which Jefferson's party was opposed. He authorized the Lewis and Clark Expedition to survey the lands of the Louisiana Purchase and find a water route to the Pacific. Jefferson's administration—as well as those of Madison and Monroe—led to the end of the Federalist Party.

Presidents 4–5—RB-904000

Thomas Jefferson, Man of Many Talents

Did You Know? The first baby born in the White House was Jefferson's grandson. At age 33, Jefferson was the youngest delegate to the Continental Congress.

Jefferson Quiz:

A. The Federalist Party believed in a strong central government. The Democratic-Republicans stressed individual liberties and wanted more power for the states. Put a D for Democratic-Republicans or an F for Federalist if the statement could apply to that party.

_____ **1.** States should disobey federal laws they dislike.

_____ **2.** All people should have complete freedom of speech.

_____ **3.** Immigration should be restricted.

_____ **4.** There should be a national bank.

_____ **5.** No more taxes!

_____ **6.** Slaves can be imported from other countries.

B. The Louisiana Purchase included all or part of these states. Identify the states outlined on the map by writing the proper number on the state.

1. Arkansas 2. Missouri

3. Iowa 4. Minnesota

5. North Dakota 6. Colorado

7. Montana 8. Wyoming

9. Nebraska 10. South Dakota

11. Oklahoma 12. Texas

13. Kansas 14. Louisiana

15. New Mexico

James Madison, Bill of Rights Author

Data & Dates

1751: Born March 16
1801: Appointed secretary of state
1812: Asked Congress to declare war against Great Britain
1836: Died June 28 at age 85, having outlived all the other Founding Fathers

Details, Details: Madison was called the father of the Constitution. He wrote the *Federalist Papers* with Alexander Hamilton to persuade voters to ratify the Constitution. He read many books about governments to prepare for the Constitutional Convention. Madison also helped frame the Bill of Rights.

Days of Youth: Jim was born a British citizen. He was the oldest son of 12 children. Seven of his brothers and sisters died while they were babies. Jim himself survived a smallpox epidemic. He liked to ride and shoot but didn't play most outdoor sports because he was small and in poor health. He loved to read and study. He attended a boarding school 70 miles from his home for five years. At the College of New Jersey, he finished the regular four years of study in only two.

He Did It: Madison served two terms. People praised him for letting others criticize his actions during the War of 1812 without fear of being jailed or put on trial. He insisted on free speech for all.

Did You Know? Madison was the smallest man to be president; he stood 5 feet 4 inches tall and barely weighed 100 pounds. He was the first president to wear long pants instead of breeches. The Madisons never returned to the White House after it was burned during the War of 1812.

Presidents 4–5—RB-904000

James Madison, Bill of Rights Author

Directions: Choose the most likely letter to fill in the blanks in the timeline.

1. **A.** The U.S. invasion of British-held Canada begins in Detroit, Michigan.
    B. The U.S. invasion of British-held Canada begins in New England.
2. **A.** The morning after the battle, a lawyer taken prisoner by the British writes "The Star-Spangled Banner," the only poem he ever wrote.
    B. The peace treaty is signed.
3. **A.** Territory is created for Indian allies of British in Ohio River Valley in U.S.
    B. Canada still has no access to the Mississippi River.
4. **A.** The Americans lose about 1 man to every 100 British soldiers.
    B. The British lose about 10 soldiers to every 1 American.

War of 1812 Timeline:

June 1812	Madison asks Congress to declare war against England. Worried about losing trade with their biggest customer, New England states refuse to participate.
July 1812	**1.** _____
Sept. 1813	Captain Perry wins control of Lake Erie for the Americans.
End of 1813	British burn Buffalo, New York.
Aug. 24, 1814	British forces push past weak U.S. troops and burn Washington, D.C.
Sept. 14, 1814	British fire cannons through the night at Baltimore's Fort McHenry.
Sept. 15, 1814	**2.** _____
Jan. 1814	British request peace talks; they are winning and think they should decide terms.
Dec. 1814	Treaty of Ghent is signed in Belgium—a continent away, across the Atlantic Ocean. Fighting ends; things are "status quo ante bellum," which means the same as before the war. **3.** _____
Jan. 8, 1815	Last battle of war fought in New Orleans. British lose more than 2,000 men; Americans lose 21. **4.** _____

James Monroe, Out Among the People

Data & Dates

1758: Born April 28
1794: Became Washington's minister to France
1803: Helped negotiate Louisiana Purchase
1831: Died July 4 at age 73

Details, Details: Upon taking the oath of office, Monroe toured the country for 15 weeks to get to know it and the people. This gave him a better knowledge of the country than any president before him. Meanwhile, the burned-out White House was still being rebuilt.

Days of Youth: As a boy, Jimmy was a skilled marksman and rider. His favorite subjects in school were math and Latin. His father died when he was 16, and he inherited the family estate.

He Did It: Monroe is best remembered for his foreign policy called the Monroe Doctrine. This warned Europe against interfering in North or South American affairs and against any attempt to establish colonies in the Americas. The Monroe Doctrine still guides U.S. actions.

Did You Know? Monroe was the last Revolutionary War officer to serve as president. He vetoed only one bill in eight years as president.

States and More States: Below is a list of the first 13 states admitted to the Union. Fill in the blanks with the circled letters to spell the two states involved in the Missouri Compromise.

1. Massachusetts
2. Pennsylvania
3. New Jersey
4. New Hampshire
5. New York
6. South Carolina
7. Georgia
8. Connecticut
9. Maryland
10. North Carolina
11. Rhode Island
12. Virginia
13. Delaware

___ ___ ___ ___ ___ ___ ___ ___   ___ ___ ___ ___ ___ ___

11

John Quincy Adams, President, Then Congressman

Data & Dates

1767: Born July 11
1794: Appointed U.S. minister to the Netherlands
1809: Appointed U.S. minister to Russia
1848: Died February 23 at age 80

Details, Details: Adams died in the U.S. Capitol Building, where he had collapsed two days earlier. His last words were: "Thank the officers of the House. This is the last of earth. I am content."

Days of Youth: Like his father, John was born in Massachusetts. When he was seven years old, fighting broke out between the British and Americans in the nearby towns of Lexington and Concord. John and his mother climbed a hill and could see smoke from the battle. They heard cannons booming. The American Revolution had begun. Three years later, when John was 10, he went with his father to France, where John Sr. served as minister to France. John lived in Europe until he was 17 and learned French very well. He later met his future wife in England.

He Did It: Adams worked hard to help American farmers and businessmen; he expanded commerce by having new roads and canals constructed.

Did You Know? Adams was elected to the U.S. House of Representatives after serving as president. After he began presenting petitions calling for the end of slavery, Congress passed a rule that slavery could not be discussed. Adams fought with great energy against this "gag rule." He believed it was wrong to restrict free speech. Eight years later he finally won the battle, and the rule was reversed.

Traveling Man: List four foreign countries where John Quincy Adams lived.

1. _____
2. _____
3. _____
4. _____

Andrew Jackson, Common Man

Data & Dates

1767: Born March 15

1796: Elected to U.S. Senate

1815: Won an important victory in War of 1812 at the Battle of New Orleans

1824: Lost a close presidential election to John Quincy Adams

1845: Died June 8 at age 78

Details, Details: Jackson's wife, Rachel, died two months after he was elected.

Days of Youth: Andy's father died before he was born. Andy was a boy during the American Revolution, and his brother Hugh died in the army. When Andy was 13, he and his brother Robert joined the army as messengers. When British soldiers charged into that part of South Carolina, Andy and Robert were taken prisoner. A British officer ordered Andy to clean his boots; when Andy refused, the officer swung his sword and cut Andy on the forehead and wrist. Andy and Robert were then taken to a prison where they got quite sick with smallpox. The boys' mother arranged for their release, but soon Andy's brother and mother both died of sickness. Andy was left an orphan.

He Did It: Jackson signed the Indian Removal Act, which forced people from five different tribes to leave their homes and move across the Mississippi River. He also put an end to the national bank, which he thought was bad for the common people.

Did You Know? Andrew Jackson was the first president born to humble circumstances; he was born in a log cabin. Previous presidents had been born to wealthy families. Jackson was also the first president to ride in a train.

The Five Civilized Tribes: The Indian Removal Act forced members of the following tribes to relocate from the southern United States to Oklahoma: Cherokee, Chickasaw, Choctaw, Creek, and Seminole. They became known as the five civilized tribes. The Cherokee nation established a constitution and published a bilingual newspaper. A Cherokee by the name of Sequoya created the first Indian alphabet. One-fourth of the 16,000 members of the tribe forced to move west died during the hard march. The Chickasaw dwelled in shelters built near streams and rivers and obtained much of their food by hunting and fishing. The Chocktaw were relatives of the Chickasaw, though they were sometimes enemies. The Chocktaw lived in cabins with thatched roofs; they grew such crops as corn, sweet potatoes, and tobacco. The Creek nation had been defeated by Andrew Jackson's army during the Creek War of 1813–14. They built a temple in each village, with a fire that was not allowed to go out. The Seminole nation had also fought against Jackson's men. Their homes were open on all sides, like a covered platform, and they hunted deer and turkeys and even turtles.

Directions: Mark each statement **True** or **False**:

1. The Mandan tribe was one of the five civilized tribes. _____

2. About 1,000 Cherokee died during the forced march. _____

3. The Chocktaw were good farmers. _____

4. Before signing the Indian Removal Act, Andrew Jackson had been friends with the five civilized tribes. _____

5. The Seminole lived in a mild climate with warm weather. _____

Martin Van Buren, Born U.S. Citizen

Data & Dates

1782: Born December 5
1812: Elected to New York state senate
1819: Wife Hannah died; Van Buren never remarried
1833: Vice president to Andrew Jackson
1840: Defeated for reelection by William Henry Harrison
1862: Died July 24 at age 79

Details, Details: Van Buren was nicknamed "the Fox" and "the Little Magician" because of his shrewd political actions. He was a good friend of Andrew Jackson and continued Jackson's policy of removing Cherokee and other Indians from their homes in Georgia to what is now Oklahoma—this sad journey is known as "The Trail of Tears."

Days of Youth: Born in New York to a middle-class family, Martin was educated by private tutors. He studied law and became an attorney at the age of 20. Martin had tastes in clothing that made some people think of him as a dandy.

He Did It: Van Buren became the first man from New York to serve in the White House. He passed the Independent Treasury Bill in an attempt to help people suffering from the economic depression of the late 1830s. He also prevented war with Britain over a logging dispute near the border of Maine and Canada.

Did You Know? Van Buren was the first president to be born in the United States after it became an independent nation. Previous presidents had been born as British subjects.

Presidents 4–5—RB-904000

Define the Terms: Check the reading to see how these terms were used. Then select the choice that best defines the term.

1. *policy*
   - **A.** trail
   - **B.** plan
   - **C.** argument
   - **D.** election

2. *shrewd*
   - **A.** funny
   - **B.** strange
   - **C.** clever
   - **D.** old

3. *middle-class*
   - **A.** those who lived in the middle of the country
   - **B.** not rich but not poor
   - **C.** not old but not young
   - **D.** people against slavery

4. *attorney*
   - **A.** politician
   - **B.** farmer
   - **C.** writer
   - **D.** lawyer

5. *dandy*
   - **A.** a man who pays close attention to the way he dresses
   - **B.** a man whose real name is Dan
   - **C.** a man who likes to ride horses
   - **D.** a fancy talker

6. *depression*
   - **A.** a period when it is difficult to earn or save money
   - **B.** a large hole in the ground
   - **C.** a time of joy and excitement
   - **D.** a war

7. *British subjects*
   - **A.** kings and queens
   - **B.** parts of sentences
   - **C.** people under British rule
   - **D.** members of the English army

Data & Dates

1773: Born February 9

1800: Elected governor of Indiana Territory

1824: Elected to U.S. Senate

1841: Died April 4 at age 68

Details, Details: Harrison became a military hero in 1811 at the Battle of Tippecanoe. His grandson Benjamin Harrison became president in 1889.

Days of Youth: William was born in Virginia and grew up on a large plantation. His family was quite wealthy. His father had signed the Declaration of Independence and served as governor of Virginia.

He Did It: Harrison was the president who served for the shortest period of time (one month) and the first president to die in office.

Did You Know? Harrison was a friend of Meriwether Lewis and William Clark. After they returned from their famous expedition in 1806, they visited Harrison in Indiana and told him all about their adventures.

Math of the Expedition: William Clark was born in 1770, and Meriwether Lewis was born in 1774. The Lewis and Clark Expedition began in May of 1804 and ended in September of 1806. Lewis died in 1809 and Clark in 1838.

1. Of Lewis, Clark, and Harrison, who was born first? _____

2. Who lived the shortest length of time? _____

3. How old was Harrison when the expedition began? _____

4. Did the expedition last more or less than two years? _____

17

John Tyler, States' Rights Supporter

Data & Dates

1790: Born March 29
1825: Became governor of Virginia
1841: Became vice president
1862: Died January 18 at age 71

Details, Details: Tyler remarried after his wife died and became the first president to marry while in office. He defended states' rights in the tradition of Jefferson. He did not seek reelection in 1844.

Days of Youth: John grew up on a plantation in Virginia; his father, a friend of Thomas Jefferson, was governor. John's mother died when he was seven.

He Did It: Tyler refused to compromise his principles to become more popular. He exercised full power as president even though some called him "His Accidency." He also signed the bill that made Texas part of the U.S.

Did You Know? Tyler was the first man to become president who was not elected to the office. He was elected vice president and became president after William Henry Harrison died.

Old Dominion: Virginia is nicknamed "Old Dominion." Use the words in this list to complete the following sentences.

Richmond   tobacco   cardinal   dogwood   Potomac

1. The state bird is the _____.
2. The _____ River forms part of Virginia's border.
3. The state capital is _____.
4. The state tree is the _____.
5. An important crop grown in Virginia is _____.

James K. Polk, Expanding the Nation

Data & Dates

1795: Born November 2
1825: Elected to the U.S. House of Representatives
1849: Died June 15 at age 53

Details, Details: Died just a few months after completing his term as president.

Days of Youth: James was born in North Carolina, but his family moved to Tennessee when he was 10. They rode in a covered wagon over bumpy roads. When they got to their new home, James was often sick and had to stay inside, but he read good books.

He Did It: Polk greatly expanded the country. Through diplomacy and war, he acquired the areas of Washington, Oregon, New Mexico, and California. For the first time, the United States stretched from sea to sea.

Did You Know? Polk had the nickname "Young Hickory" because of his friendship with Andrew Jackson. Jackson's nickname was "Old Hickory."

The Volunteer State: Before becoming president, Polk was governor of Tennessee, "the Volunteer State." Use a map to answer these questions:

1. What is the capital? (Hint: It's the city marked by a star.) _____

2. What is the name of a key river in the state? _____

3. Name one of the states that borders Tennessee on the north. _____

4. Name one of the states that borders Tennessee on the south. _____

19

Zachary Taylor, Soldier President

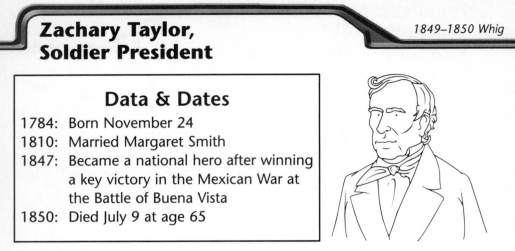

Data & Dates

1784: Born November 24
1810: Married Margaret Smith
1847: Became a national hero after winning a key victory in the Mexican War at the Battle of Buena Vista
1850: Died July 9 at age 65

Details, Details: Taylor died in office after serving for 16 months. He may have died from food poisoning after eating iced buttermilk and cherries. One of his daughters married Jefferson Davis, later president of the Confederacy.

Days of Youth: Zachary was born in Virginia and grew up on a Kentucky plantation. He learned about the military from his father, who fought in the Revolution. He became an army officer at age 24.

He Did It: Taylor was opposed to the spread of slavery, although he owned slaves. He vowed to veto the Compromise of 1850, which would allow certain territories to vote on slavery.

Did You Know? Because of his reputation as an excellent soldier, President Taylor was nicknamed "Old Rough and Ready." He felt his duty was to the military, not to politics, and he never voted in a presidential election—not even his own!

Down:

1. wife's last name

2. wife's first name

Across:

2. Taylor fought in this war.

3. state where Taylor was born

4. state where Taylor grew up

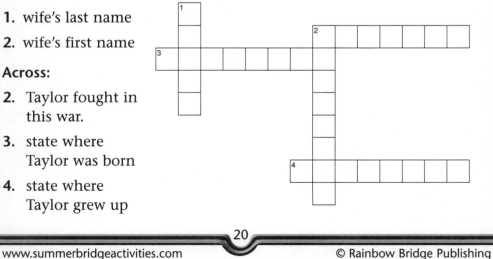

20

Millard Fillmore, Partner with Japan

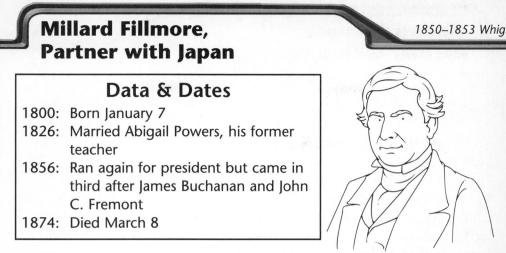

Data & Dates

1800: Born January 7
1826: Married Abigail Powers, his former teacher
1856: Ran again for president but came in third after James Buchanan and John C. Fremont
1874: Died March 8

Details, Details: Millard Fillmore became president after the death of Zachary Taylor. He was good friends with the writer Washington Irving and was the first president to have a stove and running water in the White House.

Days of Youth: Millard was born in a log cabin to a poor family. When he was 14, he was sent 100 miles from home to be an apprentice to a cloth maker. The man threatened him and treated him cruelly, but Millard defended himself. He bought his freedom and found his own way back home. He later wrote that this experience "made me feel for the weak and unprotected, and to hate the insolent tyrant in every station in life."

He Did It: Fillmore approved the Compromise of 1850, which consisted of five separate bills. The most controversial was the Fugitive Slave Act, which gave slave owners the right to kidnap runaway slaves and take them south without trials or hearings. Many northerners objected to the Fugitive Slave Act, and Fillmore quickly lost popularity. The Whig party did not nominate him for president in the election of 1852.

Did You Know? Fillmore used money from Congress to set up the first library in the White House.

21

Millard Fillmore, Partner with Japan

The Land of the Rising Sun: Fillmore was very interested in establishing trade with Japan, a country that was isolated from the rest of the world. He ordered Commodore Matthew Perry to sail to Japan and deliver diplomatic letters to the Japanese leaders. When Perry reached the bay near present-day Tokyo, Japanese officials ordered him to go to Nagasaki, the only Japanese port open to foreign vessels. Perry refused and used a show of force to negotiate. An agreement was reached. After that, ports throughout Japan were opened to ships from the United States.

Directions: Study the map below and fill in the blanks.

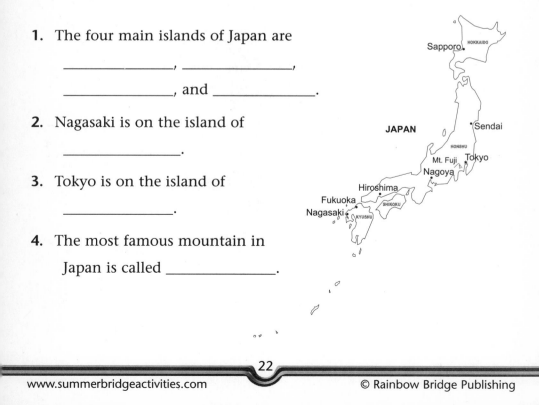

1. The four main islands of Japan are

   _____, _____,

   _____, and _____.

2. Nagasaki is on the island of

   _____.

3. Tokyo is on the island of

   _____.

4. The most famous mountain in

   Japan is called _____.

22

Franklin Pierce, Defining the Nation's Boundaries

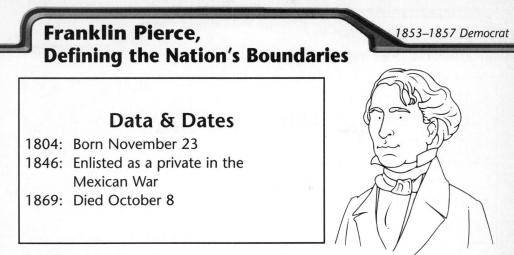

Data & Dates

1804: Born November 23
1846: Enlisted as a private in the Mexican War
1869: Died October 8

Details, Details: Born in New Hampshire; nicknamed "Handsome Frank."

Days of Youth: As a young man, Franklin became friends with the writers Henry Wadsworth Longfellow and Nathaniel Hawthorne.

He Did It: Pierce arranged to obtain a strip of land in the Southwest from Mexico. The borders of the 48 continental states have been the same since that time.

Did You Know? President Pierce and his wife, Jane, had three sons, but all three died at a young age. The last surviving son, Bennie, was killed in a train accident right before his father became president. Jane was deeply saddened by these tragedies.

The Gadsden Purchase: The map below shows the Gadsden Purchase, named after U.S. minister to Mexico, James Gadsden. The dates show when the various states joined the Union.

1. The Gadsden Purchase included land that is now in what two states? _____ _____

2. Which of the four states joined the Union first? _____

3. How many of the states joined the Union in the 20th century? _____

4. Which state joined the Union not long before Pierce became president? _____

Presidents 4–5—RB-904000

James Buchanan, Public Servant

Data & Dates

1791: Born April 23
1845: Became secretary of state under President Polk
1868: Died June 1

Details, Details: Known as "Ten-Cent Jimmy" because of his attention to detail; served as minister to Russia and later minister to Great Britain.

Days of Youth: Jimmy grew up in the beautiful farm country of Pennsylvania. His father owned a store, and Jimmy worked there. He learned to  keep careful records, a habit that endured his entire life. He was a good student and studied reading, math, English, Latin, and Greek.

He Did It: Buchanan proposed that new territories decide for themselves whether to allow slavery. This idea was quite unpopular in the northern states.

Did You Know? Buchanan was the only president who never married. His niece, Harriet Lane, served as first lady.

Pop Quiz: Cover the information above the line and answer these questions:

1. What state did Buchanan grow up in? _____

2. Name one of Buchanan's government positions before becoming president. _____

3. Buchanan's _____ served as first lady.

Abraham Lincoln, Civil War President

Data & Dates

1809: Born February 12
1842: Married Mary Todd
1846: Elected to the U.S. House of Representatives
1858: Lost a Senate race to Stephen A. Douglas
1865: Died April 15

Details, Details: Worked as a rail-splitter, a boatman, a store clerk, and a postmaster; served as a soldier in the Black Hawk War in 1832 but did not have to fight; taught himself law and became a well-respected trial attorney; became the first president to be assassinated when he was shot by John Wilkes Booth, a Southern sympathizer.

Days of Youth: Lincoln was born in a log cabin in Kentucky and nicknamed "Honest Abe." Abe borrowed books and educated himself. His mother died when he was nine. He was very sad, but when his father married Sarah Bush Johnston, Abe grew very close to her. When Abe was 19, he traveled down the Mississippi River on a flatboat. For the first time in his life, he saw slaves working in fields. He also saw slaves being bought and sold. This had a powerful effect on him and strengthened his conviction that slavery was wrong.

He Did It: In 1863, Lincoln issued the Emancipation Proclamation, which freed slaves in the areas of rebellion. The rest of the slaves did not become free until the Thirteenth Amendment to the Constitution became law after Lincoln's death.

Did You Know? At six-feet, four inches, Lincoln was the tallest president.

25

The End of Slavery: Lincoln became president after more than forty years of heated debate over slavery. The Missouri Compromise of 1820 admitted Missouri as a slave state but prohibited slavery north and west of Missouri's southern border. The Kansas-Nebraska Act of 1854 allowed territories to decide the slavery question for themselves and led to vicious fighting. Lincoln was against slavery, and when he was elected, 11 southern states seceded from the Union. Lincoln was determined to reunite the country, even if that meant fighting a war. As he feared, the Civil War began in April 1861. Over the next four years, more than 600,000 soldiers died.

Directions: Number these events in the order they happened.

_____ The Kansas-Nebraska Act is passed.

_____ Slavery is introduced to America.

_____ Abraham Lincoln is born.

_____ The Missouri Compromise is passed.

_____ The Thirteenth Amendment frees all slaves.

_____ The Civil War begins.

_____ Lincoln issues the Emancipation Proclamation.

Andrew Johnson, Veto President

Data & Dates

1808: Born December 29
1827: Married Eliza McCardle
1842: Elected to the U.S. House of
      Representatives
1856: Elected to the U.S. Senate
1875: Died July 31

Details, Details: Johnson took office after Lincoln was assassinated. He had previously served as a U.S. senator and the governor of Tennessee. When he was not nominated for a second term, he returned to his home in Tennessee. He was reelected to the U.S. Senate in 1874 but died one year later. His wife Eliza died one year after him.

Days of Youth: Andy's father died when he was three years old, and Andy lived in poverty. He wasn't able to attend school. He became an apprentice to a tailor and worked very hard to learn the trade of tailoring. He later became known as "the Tennessee Tailor."

He Did It: Johnson arranged for the purchase of Alaska from Russia. Some people thought this was foolish and called the purchase "Seward's Folly," because Secretary of State William Seward had negotiated the purchase. Many critics changed their minds after gold was discovered in Alaska.

Did You Know? President Johnson's wife, Eliza, taught him to read and write.

Presidents 4–5—RB-904000

Impeachment: Johnson and a group of Congressmen known as the Radical Republicans had serious disagreements over how to treat the South after the Civil War, during what was called Reconstruction. Like Abraham Lincoln, Johnson wanted to be lenient to the Southern states, but the radicals wanted to punish the South. Johnson frequently vetoed Congress's bills for Reconstruction.

The House of Representatives impeached Johnson. This means they put him on trial and attempted to remove him from office. The House voted for removal, but the Senate vote was one vote short, and Johnson remained in office. Controversy had erupted when Johnson fired the secretary of war. Fill in the letters to discover his last name.

1. The Radicals wanted to punish the O __ __ __ __.

2. Party that Johnson belonged to: __ __ __ __ __ __ __ O __ __

3. His wife's name was __ __ __ __ O.

4. Congressmen who opposed Johnson: Radical __ __ __ __ __ __ __ __ __ O __

5. The House put him on O __ __ __ __.

6. Alaska was called Seward's __ O __ __ __.

7. He had been governor of this state: __ __ __ O __ __ __ __ __.

Ulysses S. Grant, General in the White House

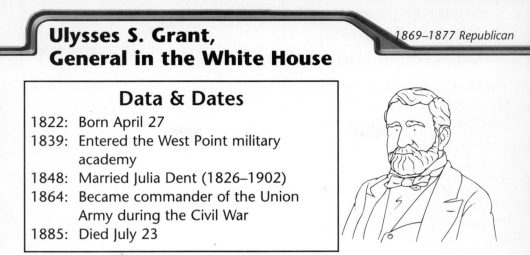

Data & Dates

1822: Born April 27
1839: Entered the West Point military academy
1848: Married Julia Dent (1826–1902)
1864: Became commander of the Union Army during the Civil War
1885: Died July 23

Details, Details: Grant served in the Mexican War under General Zachary Taylor and earned a good reputation. After the Civil War broke out, Grant quickly rose to the rank of general. In 1862 he led an attack on the Confederate post at Fort Donelson and won an important victory. Because he demanded "unconditional surrender," people began to say that was what his initials (U. S.) stood for. He was an honorable president who obeyed the laws; however, many of the people he appointed were guilty of wrongdoing. As a result, Grant was considered a poor leader, and his presidency was known for its scandals. After leaving the White House, Grant lost his life savings in bad investments.

Days of Youth: Ulysses did not like to hunt, and he did not like to work in his father's tannery, a shop where animal skins were processed into leather. Therefore, he did not think he would enjoy life at the military academy. But he liked to ride horses and became very good at it.

He Did It: In an effort to protect the African-Americans who were being terrorized by the Ku Klux Klan and other groups, Grant sent federal troops to the South and ordered many people arrested.

Did You Know? Grant became good friends with the writer Samuel Clemens, who used the pseudonym Mark Twain (1835–1910). Twain was the author of such books as *The Adventures of Tom Sawyer* and *The Adventures of Huckleberry Finn*. He encouraged Grant to write his memoirs, which Grant did, finishing the book days before he died. Royalties from the book helped support his family after his demise.

Presidents 4–5—RB-904000

Do Your English and Math Homework: Without using a dictionary, see if you can figure out what these words mean from the way they are used on the previous page. Circle your choice.

1. *pseudonym*
   A. friend
   B. fictional name used by a writer
   C. relative

2. *memoirs*
   A. autobiography
   B. novel
   C. assignment

3. *royalties*
   A. a king's family
   B. money earned from book sales
   C. taxes

4. *demise*
   A. death
   B. retirement
   C. defeat in an election

Use the information on the previous page to do these math problems:

5. Who lived the longest—Grant, his wife Julia, or Mark Twain?

   _____

6. How many years did Grant live after leaving the White House?

   _____

7. How old was Julia when Mark Twain was born? _____

8. How many years were Julia and Ulysses married? _____

Rutherford B. Hayes, Healer of the Nation

Data & Dates

1822: Born October 4
1852: Married Lucy Webb
1893: Died January 17

Details, Details: Hayes's election was controversial—he lost the popular vote, but won the electoral college by one vote. Still, he worked hard to reunite the country.

Days of Youth: He was called "Rud" as a boy. His father died before he was born; his mother was very protective because her only other son had drowned. Rud was a good student and learned Latin and Greek from a judge named Sherman Finch.

He Did It: Hayes signed an act allowing female lawyers to argue before the Supreme Court.

Did You Know? Hayes was the first president to have a telephone in the White House.

Lemonade Lucy: Lucy Hayes was the first college graduate to be first lady. With her husband's permission, she refused to serve liquor at the White House. Some people nicknamed her "Lemonade Lucy." Spell these words to discover the state where both Rutherford and Lucy were born and died.

1. President Hayes wanted women to be able to argue before the Supreme __ O __ __ __.

2. The last name of Rud's Greek and Latin tutor was __ __ __ __ O

3. Lucy was the __ O __ __ __ college graduate to be first lady.

4. Hayes used a __ __ __ __ __ __ O __ __ in the White House.

31

Presidents 4–5—RB-904000

James A. Garfield, Scholar

Data & Dates

1831: Born November 19
1862: Elected to U.S. House of
　　　Representatives
1881: A mentally ill party member named
　　　Charles Guiteau shot Garfield on July
　　　2. The president died of blood
　　　poisoning on September 19.

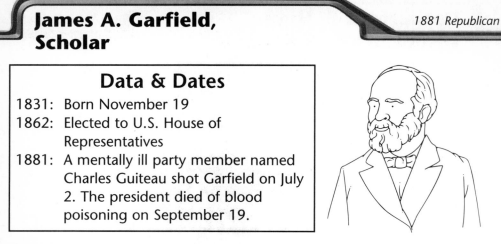

Details, Details: Garfield was opposed to slavery. He was the youngest member of the Ohio legislature at 28. He was also the youngest brigadier general in the Union Army during the Civil War.

Days of Youth: James was the baby of the family—by age eight he was running wild. He was not good at farm chores, but he loved to read. He studied hard and eventually became a college professor.

He Did It: Garfield won the election by just 10,000 votes out of 9 million cast. He made a deal with New York party boss Roscoe Conkling—promising to listen to Conkling's advice when making political appointments. Once elected, Garfield avoided scandal by appointing people based on their merit. He proved to be honest and independent. When evidence of wrongdoing was found in the U.S. Postal Service, he ordered a full investigation. He wanted reform.

Did You Know? Garfield could write with both hands at the same time.

Define the Terms: Using the "He Did It" section, draw a line from the word to the correct definition.

appointment　　　　　discovering information about something

reform　　　　　　　　correcting something that is wrong

scandal　　　　　　　　a good or valuable quality

merit　　　　　　　　　a dishonest act disgracing the people involved

wrongdoing　　　　　an immoral or illegal act

investigation　　　　　naming someone for a job

Chester A. Arthur, Reforming Civil Service

Data & Dates

1829: Born October 5
1883: Signed Pendleton Act, most important legislation of his administration
1886: Died November 18

Details, Details: Arthur was born in Vermont. He helped integrate New York City public transportation.

Days of Youth: Chester was nicknamed Chet. He moved five times during his first nine years. In college he committed the prank of dumping the school bell into the Erie Canal.

He Did It: Arthur worked for genuine reform—he refused to make payoffs and tried to stop wasteful spending.

Did You Know? He became president after James Garfield was assassinated and served without a vice president.

The Pendleton Act: The Pendleton Act set up a Civil Service Commission to oversee the merit system. People would be hired for government jobs because of their qualifications, not because of the people they knew. It was now against the law to force a government worker to give money to certain political parties. Mark **B** if the situation might have happened before the Pendleton Act. Mark **A** for after.

_____ 1. Driscol Oil Refinery made a voluntary contribution to the Democratic Party.

_____ 2. Post Office workers learned they would be required to give $5 to the Republican Party.

_____ 3. When Tahlia finished college, she got a job at the courthouse.

_____ 4. Carl Morris knew Senator Gregory. That's how he got his government job.

33

Grover Cleveland, Two-Times President

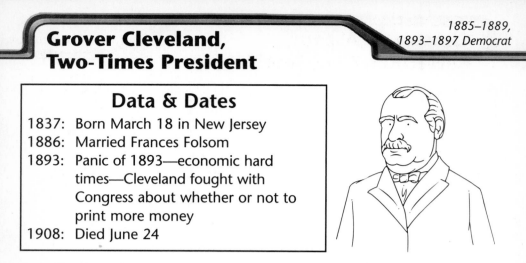

Data & Dates

1837: Born March 18 in New Jersey
1886: Married Frances Folsom
1893: Panic of 1893—economic hard times—Cleveland fought with Congress about whether or not to print more money
1908: Died June 24

Details, Details: Many words can be used to describe Cleveland, including hard worker, honest, detailed, blunt, and hot-tempered. He served as mayor of Buffalo and governor of New York.

Days of Youth: Cleveland was called Stephen as a child. He did chores like chopping wood, weeding the garden, and babysitting younger brothers and sisters. Swimming and fishing were his favorite sports. He believed in making good use of his time. At 14 he worked as an apprentice for one dollar a week. Later, he went west to study law.

He Did It: Cleveland believed in "hands-off" government: people support the government, not the other way around. He played little role in shaping legislation, although he did sign the Interstate Commerce Act in 1893. He also made sure that railroads charged "reasonable and just" rates.

Did You Know? Cleveland was the first Democratic president since the Civil War. He was the only president to serve two non-consecutive terms. His was the first wedding of a president to take place in the White House. His wife, at age 21, was the youngest first lady in history. He ignored public and political opinion—this cost him reelection twice.

Grover Cleveland, Two-Times President

Idioms: An idiom is a common expression that means something different from what it seems to mean. Draw a line from each idiom to its meaning.

hands-off   do the right thing

hot-tempered   let events take their own course

stand for something   quick to anger

Cause and Effect: Railroads had been allowed to charge shippers and passengers what they wished. This often resulted in outrageously high prices and favoritism. Rebates to big corporations became a common practice. The Interstate Commerce Act ensured that railroads charged fair rates. The Interstate Commerce Commission, or ICC, was created to oversee the railroads and was the first regulatory agency created by Congress.

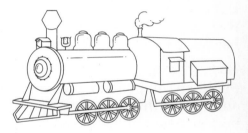

Mark **C** for something that caused or led to the Interstate Commerce Act and **E** for something that was the result of the Interstate Commerce Act. One item should have both a C and an E.

1. High prices and favoritism were typical.   _____

2. Corporations were given rebates.   _____

3. Congress created the ICC.   _____

4. Railroads set their own prices.   _____

5. Railroads had someone to watch over them.   _____

Benjamin Harrison, Above Suspicion

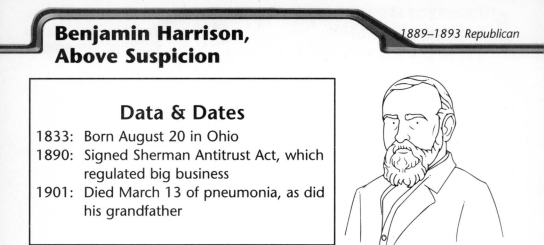

Data & Dates

1833: Born August 20 in Ohio

1890: Signed Sherman Antitrust Act, which regulated big business

1901: Died March 13 of pneumonia, as did his grandfather

Details, Details: Harrison was called the "human iceberg" because he was very formal and uncomfortable with people. However, he was a hard worker and paid attention to details. He was also incorruptible.

Days of Youth: Ben was seven when his grandfather was elected president. As a child he fetched wood and water and fed horses and animals on the farm. He liked to swim, hunt, and fish. After he became a lawyer, he served in the Civil War.

He Did It: Harrison won the presidency with a majority of electoral votes even though his opponent, Cleveland, won the popular vote.

Did You Know? Harrison was the first president to use electricity in the White House; he was also the only president to be the grandson of another president (William Henry Harrison).

Benjamin Harrison, Animal Lover: President Harrison had plenty of pets at the White House. Circle the four pets you can find in the word search. Two of the pets were unusual: one had horns and pulled the grandchildren in a cart around the White House lawn.

```
m  i  h  e  n  a  w  w  t  f
q  b  b  m  q  m  n  p  b  s
g  o  m  q  u  n  k  x  s  t
m  n  d  o  g  s  k  f  a  v
h  q  h  z  m  d  s  k  l  o
q  o  h  t  a  o  g  o  c  s
i  e  r  f  y  r  p  d  p  b
w  b  u  s  s  h  k  x  l  o
m  s  p  r  e  t  x  s  q  r
l  g  l  o  r  n  s  k  j  t
```

William McKinley, Veteran of the Civil War

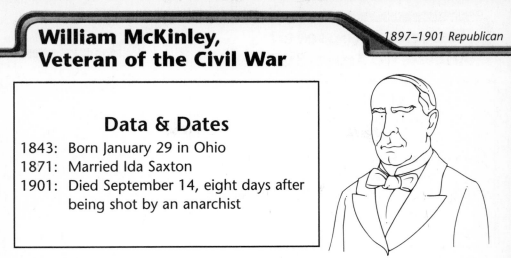

Data & Dates

1843: Born January 29 in Ohio
1871: Married Ida Saxton
1901: Died September 14, eight days after being shot by an anarchist

Details, Details: McKinley had a warm, friendly way that could make an angry person smile.

Days of Youth: Bill was the seventh of nine children; he was given the chores of chopping wood and driving the cows to pasture. He liked to play army wearing a paper hat and waving a wooden sword. He loved fishing, skating, horseback riding, and a good game of marbles.

He Did It: McKinley was a hands-off president. This resulted in the development of huge business trusts.

Did You Know? McKinley was the last president to have fought in the Civil War, the first to use a telephone to campaign, the fifth to die in office, and the third to be assassinated.

Numbers, Numbers: Fill in the blanks with one of the choices at the right.

1. _____ of _____ children   nine

2. _____ president of the United States   fifth

3. _____ president to use a phone to campaign   third

4. _____ president to die in office   seventh

5. Died _____ days after being shot   first

6. _____ president to be assassinated   eight

                                                                twenty-fifth

Presidents 4–5—RB-904000

Theodore Roosevelt, Energetic Trust-Buster

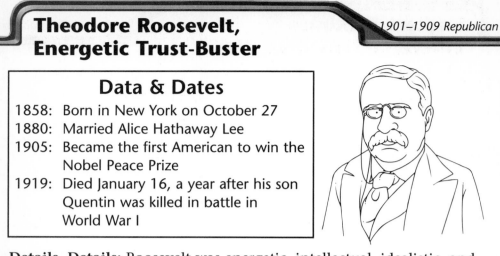

Data & Dates

1858: Born in New York on October 27

1880: Married Alice Hathaway Lee

1905: Became the first American to win the Nobel Peace Prize

1919: Died January 16, a year after his son Quentin was killed in battle in World War I

Details, Details: Roosevelt was energetic, intellectual, idealistic, and determined. He became president after McKinley was assassinated.

Days of Youth: Teddy was schooled at home. He was a sickly child with asthma. As a result, when he grew up he took up sports to improve his health. He attended Harvard University, where he competed on the boxing team. He married his childhood playmate.

He Did It: He broke up huge trusts (a *trust* is a company that owns many others) and became known as a "trust-buster." He helped settle labor disputes and increased safety standards for the preparation of food and medicine. He established the role of the United States as an international police power.

Did You Know? Roosevelt sometimes read three books a night. The teddy bear was named after him. At 42 he was the youngest man to ever be president. He was the first president to fly in an airplane, ride in a car, or dive in a submarine. His children were called "The White House Gang." They often slid down the stairs on metal trays and once took a pony upstairs in the elevator to the bedroom.

38

Theodore Roosevelt, Energetic Trust-Buster

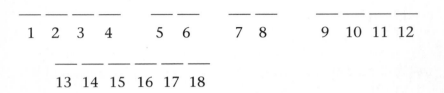

"A Man for All Seasons": This phrase offers a good description of Theodore Roosevelt. Fill in the blanks with the underlined letters to find what the phrase means.

__ __ __ __   __ __   __ __   __ __ __ __
1 2 3 4   5 6   7 8   9 10 11 12

__ __ __ __ __ __
13 14 15 16 17 18

<u>A</u>sthmatic; <u>b</u>oxer; horseback-rider; cattle rancher; <u>l</u>egislator; reader, writer, and <u>e</u>nvironmentalist; cowboy; politician; <u>t</u>rust-buster; <u>ou</u>tstanding teacher; assistant secretary of the Navy; <u>d</u>ad to six energetic children; jogger; hunter; <u>o</u>fficer with Civil Service Commission; <u>m</u>ountain climber; <u>a</u>ctive in world affairs; head of New York City Police Board; <u>N</u>obel Prize winner; <u>y</u>oungest president; <u>t</u>ennis player; diplomat; weight-lifter and <u>h</u>iker; <u>i</u>ntelligent; Rough Rider; <u>n</u>egotiator; man of action; governor; vice president; <u>s</u>wimmer

39

Presidents 4–5—RB-904000

William Howard Taft, Supreme Court Justice

Data & Dates

1857: Born September 15
1913: Was president when the 16th and
17th Amendments were ratified,
which allowed for a federal income
tax and for people instead of legisla-
tors to elect senators
1930: Died March 8

Details, Details: Taft was a brilliant man. He was governor of the Philippines and served as secretary of war to Roosevelt. He also over-saw construction of the Panama Canal.

Days of Youth: Bill attended public schools and graduated second in his class at Yale.

He Did It: Taft created the Department of Labor and took control of railroad freight fares. He became a Supreme Court justice eight years after serving as president—and was the only man to do both.

Did You Know? Taft was the heaviest president. He began the tradi-tion of the president throwing out the first ball on opening day of the baseball season.

Rub-A-Dub-Dub: Taft weighed 332 pounds. He put in a new tub for himself that was big enough to fit four men.

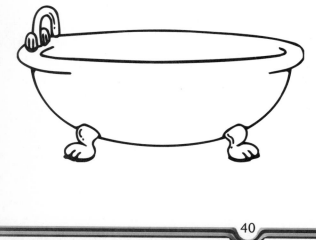

How many pounds would each of those men have weighed if the four men made up one President Taft?

_____

Woodrow Wilson, Responsibly Moral

Data & Dates

1856: Born December 28
1913: Federal Reserve Act passed to stabilize money and credit
1917: War declared on April 7
1924: Died February 3

Details, Details: He was a professor, a lawyer, a persuasive speaker, and an author; one book he wrote was translated into many languages and had 29 editions. Wilson won a three-way presidential race in 1912 against President Taft and former president Theodore Roosevelt.

Days of Youth: He was a boy during the Civil War. Up until he went to law school he was known as "Tommy." After that, he began using his middle name, Woodrow. He had dyslexia, a learning disorder, and could not read well until he was 11. He learned to speak persuasively from his father, a Presbyterian minister, and became a star debater at Princeton University.

He Did It: Wilson established the Federal Reserve system and promoted the eight-hour workday. He helped establish the League of Nations, which became the United Nations after World War II. This earned him the Nobel Peace Prize.

Did You Know? As a professor at Princeton, Wilson taught classes of more than 400 students. He was voted most popular professor year after year. He was the first president to hold press conferences and speak on the radio. Two of his three daughters were married in the White House.

Woodrow Wilson, Responsibly Moral

Fractions and Rations: During World War I, people in the U.S. were asked to ration many things, or use things sparingly. Rationing helped provide scarce items to the troops fighting the war. President Wilson and his family did their part. To find out what the First Family rationed, solve the math problems below. Then match the four answers with the four corresponding items in the list. Write the name of each item next to the "piece of the pie" it goes with.

$3/4 \times 1/6 =$ 1/2 gasoline

$7/8 \times 2/7 =$ 3/8 blankets

$2/3 \times 3/4 =$ 1/16 sweets

$1/2 \times 1/8 =$ 1/8 meat

                                    3/4 water

                                    2/3 soap

                                    1/4 wheat

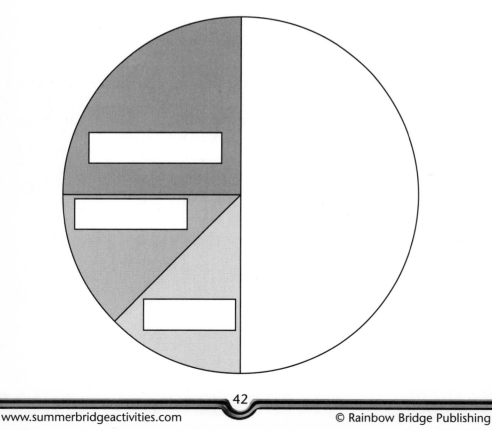

42

Warren G. Harding, Civil Rights Supporter

Data & Dates

1865: Born November 2
1921: Was the first president to ride to his swearing-in ceremony in an automobile
1923: Died August 2, after becoming ill on a speaking tour

Details, Details: Harding was the sixth president to die in office; his health failed at midterm. He also served as senator from and governor of Ohio.

Days of Youth: Warren was born seven months after the end of the Civil War. He was the oldest of eight children. He learned poetry at age 4 and was a good speller and writer by age 10.

He Did It: He began a cross-country speaking tour to restore confidence in his administration.

Did You Know? Harding was elected on his 56th birthday. His presidency is ranked one of the worst in history because of corruption in the administration, though he was not involved.

A Big Victory: "It wasn't a landslide, it was an earthquake." When Harding was elected, he captured 60 percent of the popular vote, the greatest presidential victory in history. These were the results:

Harding   Cox
16,152,200   9,147,353

1. What was the difference in the popular vote? _____
2. Round the difference to the nearest million. _____

Calvin Coolidge, Integrity in Office

Data & Dates

1872: Born July 4
1895: Graduated cum laude (with honors)
         from Amherst College
1933: Died January 5

Details, Details: A man of few words, Coolidge was nicknamed "Silent Cal." He was honest and self-reliant with a witty sense of humor. He served as mayor of Northhampton, Massachusetts, and senator from and governor of Massachusetts.

Days of Youth: Cal was a shy and quiet boy who had red hair and freckles. He loved to make maple syrup. He had to cut firewood, mend fences, and drive the cattle to pasture. Cal loved to ice skate, swim, and fish. He lost his mother at the age of 12.

He Did It: Coolidge twice vetoed a farm bill to set prices for agricultural goods. He reorganized the FBI, cut taxes, and reduced the national debt.

Did You Know? He was the only president to be sworn in by his father.

A Man of Few Words: Coolidge was famous for using few words to say something. Read the quote below about Coolidge and see how few words you can use to say the same thing.

> "His character is as firm as the mountains of his native state. Like them his head's above the clouds and he stands unshaken amid the tumult and the storm."

Now write your version:

_____

_____

_____

_____

Herbert C. Hoover, Great Humanitarian

1929–1933 Republican

Data & Dates
1874: Born August 10
1917: Named President Wilson's food administrator; nicknamed "Food Czar," he controlled the country's food supply
1928: Elected president by unheard of majority of 6 million votes
1964: Died October 20 at age 90

Details, Details: Hoover was hardheaded, thrifty, and efficient. He was raised a Quaker and learned patience, responsibility to the community, and a belief in individual worth. These qualities helped him handle the task of feeding the country of Belgium during World War I. Hoover was a progressive businessman who believed government should help business owners and workers work together.

Days of Youth: He was known as "Bert" as a boy. Bert was a hard worker and did chores like picking potato bugs for one penny for every hundred. He was orphaned at age nine. He turned from a shy boy into a reserved adult who kept his feelings to himself; some thought him cold and blunt. Herbert graduated from Stanford University as a mining engineer, a job that earned him millions. He and his wife, Lou, both learned Chinese.

He Did It: Hoover gave loans to banks and businesses after the stock market crash started the Great Depression; he did not give help directly to citizens because he did not believe in government welfare. Some blamed him for the Depression. He signed the Agricultural Marketing Act, helping farmers join together to store, sell, and ship their crops. The act also formed the Federal Farm Board to control the food supply.

Did You Know? Hoover lived longer than any president after leaving office—31 years.

Presidents 4–5—RB-904000

Herbert C. Hoover, Great Humanitarian

Crossword Puzzle: President Hoover's personality made it hard for him to be elected a second time. Read the selection on the previous page and find words describing Hoover that fit the meanings below. Use them to fill in the puzzle.

Down

1. speak honestly with no concern for others' feelings
3. put up with delays
4. does not show feeling
5. not comfortable with people
8. use money or supplies wisely

Across

2. unfriendly
6. stubborn
7. someone who helps suffering people
9. can be trusted
10. work without wasting time

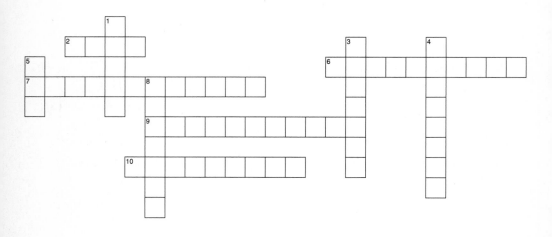

Franklin D. Roosevelt, President of Action

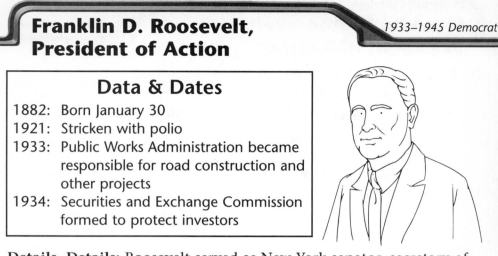

Data & Dates

1882: Born January 30

1921: Stricken with polio

1933: Public Works Administration became responsible for road construction and other projects

1934: Securities and Exchange Commission formed to protect investors

Details, Details: Roosevelt served as New York senator, secretary of the navy to Woodrow Wilson, and governor of New York. He became president during the Great Depression.

Days of Youth: An only child, after he was born he had no name for seven weeks until his parents finally chose one. He liked to swim, garden, ride his pony, and collect things—especially stamps. By the time he was an adult, his stamp collection had become world famous.

He Did It: President Roosevelt worked to end the Depression with a take-charge attitude. He signed bills that formed the Civilian Conservation Corps, which provided jobs improving national parks, and the Tennessee Valley Authority, which helped construct dams and power plants. He also signed the Emergency Banking Act, which provided loans to people. FDR explained all of these changes to the American people over radio broadcasts he called "Fireside Chats."

Did You Know? FDR was the only president to serve three terms and be elected to a fourth, making his the longest presidency in U.S. history. His fifth cousin, Teddy Roosevelt, was the 26th president. He married his distant cousin Eleanor Roosevelt, whose uncle was Teddy Roosevelt. FDR was also the first president to be on TV.

Franklin D. Roosevelt, President of Action

Data & Dates

1935: Social Security Act passed
1935: Federal Deposit Insurance Corporation created
1939: World War II began
1945: Died April 12 while serving fourth term as president

Initials and More Initials: Franklin Delano Roosevelt became known by the initials FDR. The beginning of his presidency brought a number of reforms to help deal with the Depression. During that time, called "Roosevelt's Hundred Days," Congress passed 14 bills. FDR called them the "New Deal." Listed below are the initials of some of the bills passed while FDR was president. Reread the passage on FDR to find what the initials stand for. Then fill in the blanks.

1. EBA

_____

2. CCC

_____

3. PWA

_____

4. TVA

_____

5. FDIC

_____

6. SEC

_____

7. SS

_____

Harry S. Truman, "The Buck Stops Here"

Data & Dates

1884: Born May 8
1919: Fought in World War I
1919: Married Bess Wallace
1944: Elected vice president
1972: Died December 26

Details, Details: Truman was born in Missouri and was the only 20th century president not to attend college (although he became well educated on his own). He served for 10 years in the U.S. Senate and became president after the death of Franklin Roosevelt. Truman brought World War II to an end by dropping atomic bombs on Japan. Later he announced the "Truman Doctrine," which meant the U.S. would help any country trying to fight Communism. Following his own doctrine, Truman sent troops to defend South Korea from Communist aggression; the Korean War lasted from 1950 to 1953.

Days of Youth: Harry learned to read by the time he was five years old. He loved riding a pony and playing in the fields on his grandfather's farm. Some of the other children made fun of him because he wore glasses at a young age. But he became a very good student.

He Did It: Truman always took responsibility for his actions. The phrase "passing the buck" means blaming someone else. Truman was famous for saying "the buck stops here," which meant he would not blame others for his decisions.

Did You Know? In 1948, Truman ran for reelection against Thomas Dewey. The polls predicted that Dewey would win. Late in the evening of election day, it still looked like Dewey would win. The *Chicago Daily Tribune* even printed a newspaper article saying Dewey had won. But hours after the newspaper was printed, the count of votes showed that Truman had won. A famous picture shows Truman holding up a copy of the newspaper.

Presidents 4–5—RB-904000

Harry S. Truman, "The Buck Stops Here"

"Dewey Defeats Truman": The *Chicago Daily Tribune* newspaper made a big mistake when it published this headline. See if you can find four mistakes in the following imaginary newspaper article. Write why each is a mistake on the lines below.

Harry Truman was born in Missouri. He had trouble in school when he was young. He was the kind of person who wanted to take responsibility for his actions. He played on the college football team. He served for 10 years in the U.S. Senate. He served as vice president to Franklin Roosevelt. The Truman Doctrine was a program to help the poor. Truman helped South Korea, although the Korean War started before Truman became president.

1. _____.

2. _____.

3. _____.

4. _____.

Dwight D. Eisenhower, World War II Hero

Data & Dates

1890: Born October 14
1916: Married Mamie Geneva Doud
1969: Died March 28

Details, Details: Eisenhower was a skilled general who commanded Allied forces during World War II. He made key decisions that helped defeat Germany and Italy.

Days of Youth: Ike, as Eisenhower was called, loved to play football, and he also loved to read about ancient battles.

He Did It: Eisenhower appointed Earl Warren chief justice of the Supreme Court in 1953. The next year, the Supreme Court declared segregation (forcing whites and blacks to stay separate) illegal. Governor Faubus of Arkansas refused to obey the law and prevented African-American students from attending an all-white school. A court ordered Faubus to let the students attend, but he refused to protect them. Eisenhower sent federal troops to protect the children so they could attend. These brave students were known as "the Little Rock Nine."

Did You Know? Just weeks after being elected in 1952, Eisenhower made a secret trip to Korea to decide how to handle the Korean War after he became president.

Directions: Number these events in the correct order.

_____ The Little Rock Nine safely attend school.

_____ Faubus refuses to obey the law.

_____ Eisenhower sends in federal troops.

_____ Supreme Court rules segregation illegal.

51

John F. Kennedy,
Young Senator from Massachusetts

Data & Dates

1917: Born May 29
1941: Served in World War II
1952: Elected to the U.S. Senate
1953: Married Jacqueline Bouvier, then 24
1963: Assassinated on November 22

Details, Details: Kennedy was nicknamed JFK. He never lost an election. JFK was famous for saying, "Ask not what your country can do for you—ask what you can do for your country."

Days of Youth: Jack, as Kennedy was called as a boy, had a big brother named Joe. Joe excelled in both sports and studies. Jack tried hard to compete with Joe but was often sick as a child. He lived in Joe's shadow until Joe died in World War II.

He Did It: When Kennedy discovered that the Soviet Union was building nuclear missile bases in Cuba, he ordered Soviet Premier Khrushchev to remove them. Khrushchev agreed to do so, and war was narrowly avoided.

Did You Know? President Kennedy was the youngest man ever elected president, at the age of 43 (Teddy Roosevelt was 42 when he became president after McKinley's assassination). Kennedy was also the youngest president to die in office, at age 46.

The Death of the President: In November 1963, President and Jacqueline Kennedy flew to Dallas. As they were riding in a car with Texas governor John Connally and his wife, Nellie, shots rang out. A young man named Lee Harvey Oswald had fatally wounded the president. Governor Connally was also shot, but he survived. Shortly after the president's death, vice president Lyndon B. Johnson was sworn in as president. Oswald was not brought to trial because two days after the assassination he was shot and killed by a nightclub owner by the name of Jack Ruby. Ruby used a revolver, but his victim had used a rifle. Ruby had liked Kennedy and had been very upset about his death. Ever since that time, controversy has surrounded President Kennedy's death, with some people believing that Oswald was innocent or that others conspired with him.

Directions: Draw a line to match the person with the detail that describes him or her. Use your brain power to figure out correct answers even if the detail was not discussed above.

Jacqueline Kennedy   shot and killed the assassin

Lee Harvey Oswald   ran for reelection the year after JFK died

John Connally   was in surgery when Kennedy died

Nellie Connally   became a widow at a young age

Jack Ruby   fired three shots with a rifle

Lyndon B. Johnson   spoke to JFK right before shots rang out

Presidents 4–5—RB-904000

Lyndon B. Johnson, Advocate for the Poor

1963–1969 Democrat

Data & Dates

1908: Born August 27
1937: Elected to the U.S. House of Representatives
1948: Elected to the U.S. Senate
1934: Married Claudia Taylor, who was nicknamed Lady Bird
1973: Died January 22

Details, Details: There were 16,000 U.S. troops in Vietnam by the time Johnson became president. In 1964 he requested and received authority from Congress to send more troops. He did this in an attempt to stop the spread of Communism. By 1967 there were 400,000 American soldiers in Vietnam. Throughout the United States, people protested the war. Johnson became very discouraged and decided not to seek reelection in 1968. Ironically, a formal peace treaty in Vietnam was signed in 1973, just five days after Johnson died.

Days of Youth: Young Lyndon had three younger sisters and one younger brother. They lived on a ranch, and Lyndon organized the others to do chores. He often wore a nice shirt and tie to school, even though no one else did. He was taller than his classmates and got good grades; he was interested in government from an early age.

He Did It: Johnson developed many programs, including Medicaid and Medicare, to help the poor and the elderly. He also established a preschool for poor children called Head Start. Lady Bird also promoted programs to help poor people. Johnson's war on poverty became known as "The Great Society."

Did You Know? There are many similarities between the 17th president and the 36th president. Both were from the South; both were named Johnson; each became president after the previous president was assassinated; Lincoln had been elected in 1860 and Kennedy in 1960. Andrew Johnson left office in 1869, and Lyndon Johnson left in 1969.

www.summerbridgeactivities.com　　　　© Rainbow Bridge Publishing

Lyndon B. Johnson, Advocate for the Poor

True or False: Mark each sentence **T** for true or **F** for false.

____ **1.** When he was a boy, Lyndon did most of the farm chores himself.

____ **2.** Johnson decided not to seek reelection in 1968 because people did not like his programs for the poor.

____ **3.** Johnson served in both the U.S. House of Representatives and the Senate.

____ **4.** Johnson served two full terms as president.

____ **5.** Johnson sent the first U.S. troops to Vietnam.

____ **6.** Johnson became president after Kennedy was assassinated.

____ **7.** Lyndon was a good student when he was young.

Presidents 4–5—RB-904000

Richard M. Nixon, Diplomat

Data & Dates

1913: Born January 9
1940: Married Pat Ryan
1952: Elected vice president under Eisenhower
1960: Lost a close presidential election to John F. Kennedy
1994: Died April 22

Details, Details: Nixon served in the navy during World War II. He was elected to Congress in 1946 when he defeated prominent congressman Jerry Voorhis. He later said that nothing matched the excitement of his first election.

Days of Youth: Richard's parents were Quakers, or members of the Society of Friends. The Quakers worked hard and did not believe in war. They also objected to alcoholic drinks, music, and dancing. Richard was a serious child who learned to read at an early age. He dreamed of being a railroad engineer. When he was 12, his 7-year-old brother, Arthur, died. This made Richard very sad.

He Did It: In 1971, President Nixon announced plans to visit Communist China. This surprised the world because Nixon had long fought against Communism and because the U.S. and China had not enjoyed cordial relations for many years. But Nixon was a skilled diplomat, and the visit was quite successful.

Did You Know?
Nixon's daughter married David Eisenhower, grandson of President Eisenhower.

Richard M. Nixon, Diplomat

The Watergate Scandal: In June of 1972, five burglars were arrested for breaking into the Democratic Party headquarters at the Watergate Hotel. One of the burglars later claimed the Nixon administration had organized the break-in and several other illegal activities. Nixon denied this, but reporters for the *Washington Post* continued to investigate the story. One by one, Nixon's aides began to resign. Several were charged with crimes. Then it became known that Nixon had tape-recorded many of his conversations in the White House. Legal battles over the tapes followed, until the Supreme Court ordered Nixon to turn over the tapes. The tapes showed that Nixon had acted illegally to keep secrets. In August of 1974, when it became obvious that Congress would likely vote to remove him from office, Nixon resigned. President Ford pardoned him to help the nation move forward.

Directions: For each pair of statements, identify the cause with **C** and the effect with **E**.

_____ the police arrive at the Watergate

_____ someone sees burglars in an office

_____ existence of the tapes becomes known

_____ lawyers argue over tapes

_____ Nixon turns over tapes

_____ Supreme Court reaches decision on tapes

_____ Ford concludes a trial might last two years

_____ Ford pardons Nixon

Gerald R. Ford,
First President Not Elected

1974–1977 Republican

Data & Dates

1913: Born July 14 in Omaha, Nebraska
1935: Graduated from the University of Michigan
1948: Married Betty Bloomer, who was born in Illinois
1973: Appointed vice president by Richard Nixon

Details, Details: Ford was ambidextrous (both right- and left-handed) and would change hands depending on his preference. When Vice President Spiro Agnew resigned in 1973, President Nixon appointed Gerald Ford as vice president. (The 25th Amendment gives the president this power.)

Days of Youth: Jerry liked sports and fishing. He was a good student and earned the rank of Eagle Scout. He especially liked football and became a star football player at the University of Michigan.

He Did It: To help the nation recover from the Watergate scandal, President Ford pardoned Richard Nixon. After his resignation, Nixon returned to his home in California.

Did You Know? During a three-week period in 1975, two different young women tried to shoot President Ford. Fortunately, he was not injured.

Name the State

1. Nixon's home: _____

2. Betty's birthplace: _____

3. Jerry's birthplace: _____

4. Football team: _____

Jimmy E. Carter, Peacemaker

Data & Dates

1924: Born October 1
1946: Graduated from the U.S. Naval Academy and married Rosalyn Smith
1994: Helped negotiate peace in Haiti

Details, Details: Carter ran the family peanut business for several years.

Days of Youth: When Jimmy was young, he worked very hard in the cotton fields. He liked to fish and read for fun; when he was only 12, he read a big book called *War and Peace*.

He Did It: In 1978, Carter invited President Sadat of Egypt and Prime Minister Begin of Israel to the United States for peace negotiations. Egypt and Israel had been enemies for 30 years. With Carter's help, a historic peace agreement was reached.

Did You Know? After leaving office, Carter has devoted his time to helping others. Along with helping countries live peacefully, he often brings his tools to help build houses for poor people.

The Peach State: Jimmy Carter was born in Plains, Georgia, and was later governor of that state. Study the map and answer **True** or **False**.

1. Part of Georgia borders the Gulf of Mexico. _____

2. The capital is Macon. _____

3. Alabama is to the west. _____

4. Going north from different parts of Georgia can lead you into three different states. _____

Presidents 4–5—RB-904000

Ronald W. Reagan, From Hollywood to the Capital

Data & Dates

1911: Born February 6
1937: Began his acting career at Warner Brothers studio
1952: Married Nancy Davis
1981: Wounded in an assassination attempt but recovered
2004: Died June 5

Hint: Watch out for spelling errors on this page.

Details, Details: Reagan was called "the Great Communicater" because of his ease with the press and his ability to convey his ideas. To save money after he became governor of California, he had secretaries use old stationery by crossing out the old governor's name and typing in his. He loved jelly beans and often passed them around at meetings.

Days of Youth: "Dutch" Reagan, as he was called as a boy, grew up in Illnois. His mother taught him to read before he was five years old. His family lived near the Rock River for a time, and Dutch loved to swim and canoe in the summer and ice skate in the winter. He also loved to explore the woods along the bank of the river.

He Did It: Reagan apointed the first woman to the U.S. Supreme Court. Her name is Sandra Day O'Connor.

Did You Know? At age 69, Reagan was the oldest person to become president. He was a famous acter before becoming a politician in the 1960s. One of his best known moovies, *Knute Rockne—All American*, was about a famous football coach. Reagan played George Gipp. When Gipp's character became quite ill in the movie, Reagan said one of his best loved lines: "Ask the boys to go in there and win just once for the Gipper." While he was president, people often called Reagan "the Gipper."

www.summerbridgeactivities.com

Spelling Test: There are five words spelled incorrectly on the previous page. Can you find them? Below, write each word you found; then write the correct spelling.

1. _____   _____

2. _____   _____

3. _____   _____

4. _____   _____

5. _____   _____

Presidents 4–5—RB-904000

George Bush, Experienced Leader

Data & Dates

1924: Born June 12
1942: Enlisted in the navy and served in World War II
1945: Married Barbara Pierce
1976: Appointed director of the Central Intelligence Agency

Details, Details: Bush served as vice president to Ronald Reagan.

Days of Youth: George was reared in a wealthy family, but his parents taught him to share with others. He gave away half of his treats so often that his family nicknamed him "have half." He loved to frolic on the rocky coast of Maine, where the family took vacations.

He Did It: After Saddam Hussein, the dictator of Iraq, ordered the invasion of Kuwait, Bush launched Operation Desert Storm to fight Iraq. Iraqi troops were driven out of Kuwait in six weeks.

Did You Know? Bush's plane was shot down in World War II. Although he was injured, he floated in the ocean on a rubber raft until a submarine rescued him.

Synonym, synonym: Circle the word with similar meaning.

1. reared: raised   taught   punished
2. frolic: work   play   sit
3. enlisted in: joined   ignored   liked
4. launched: brought   gambled   started

Data & Dates

1946: Born August 19
1973: Graduated from Yale Law School
1975: Married Hillary Rodham
1976: Became attorney general of Arkansas
1978: Elected governor of Arkansas

Details, Details: During his presidency, Bill Clinton was accused of perjury and obstruction of justice. He was impeached and tried before Congress. However, he was acquitted.

Days of Youth: Billy's dad died in a car accident before Billy was born. He lived with his grandparents for a time while his mom studied to become a nurse. One Thanksgiving, Billy's mom sent him to the store; he came home with a poor boy he had met at the store. The boy had a nice dinner with Billy's family. Billy frequently showed this kind of concern for other people. Later, Billy learned how to play the saxophone and played so well that he was named to the all-state first band.

He Did It: Clinton helped promote free trade with Canada and Mexico with the North American Free Trade Agreement. The U.S. economy prospered under Clinton. He began balancing the budget, the first time this had been done in 40 years.

Did You Know? Clinton was the first president born after World War II. He was part of the "baby boomer" generation. At age 32, he became the nation's youngest governor. However, after raising taxes to improve schools and roads, he lost his bid for reelection. But he was determined to be governor again. He worked very hard and was reelected. He served four consecutive terms as Arkansas's governor. People called him "the comeback kid."

© Rainbow Bridge Publishing

The Meeting of Two Presidents: In high school Bill joined a youth program called Boys' State. He ran for Boys' State senator and won, which meant he would go to Boys' Nation in Washington, D.C. In 1963, the young men went to the White House, and young Bill shook hands with President John F. Kennedy, who had been in office since 1961. It was a great moment for Bill; from that point on, he knew he wanted to go into politics.

1. When the two presidents met, how long had Kennedy been president? _____

2. Kennedy was born in 1917. How much older was he than Clinton? _____

3. How many years after he met Kennedy did Clinton become president? _____

4. Who was younger when he became president, Kennedy or Clinton? _____

George W. Bush, Son of a President

Data & Dates

1946: Born July 6
1977: Married Laura Welch
1994: Elected governor of Texas
2001: Changed focus of administration after terrorist attacks of September 11

Details, Details: Bush was the first son of a president to become president himself since John Quincy Adams took office in 1825.

Days of Youth: When George was six, his grandfather became a U.S. senator. George liked fishing and other outdoor activities. He loved playing baseball and wanted to be a star baseball player when he grew up. He later became an owner of the Texas Rangers baseball team.

He Did It: After the World Trade Center and the Pentagon were attacked, President Bush led a war against terrorism. He sent soldiers to Afghanistan and Iraq to stop future attacks on the United States.

Did You Know? Bush was the first president to be the father of twins; his and Laura's twin girls are named Jenna and Barbara.

George W. Bush, Son of a President

The Close Election of 2000: In this election, George W. Bush, then governor of Texas, ran against Democratic candidate Al Gore, vice president to Bill Clinton. As the votes were counted on the night of November 7, it became clear that the election was very close. The electoral votes were almost evenly divided. The winner of Florida would win the election. However, the voting was extremely close, and there were several problems in Florida. Some of the machines did not count the ballots properly, and some of the ballots were not properly punched. Politicians and lawyers on both sides argued about how or whether votes should be recounted. The case finally went to the Supreme Court, which stopped the recount. Bush was declared the winner, getting 271 electoral votes to Gore's 266. Gore lost, even though he received more popular votes than Bush.

Bush ran against Democrat John Kerry in 2004 and won again, but it was not as close as the famous and controversial election of 2000.

Directions: Use these clues to complete the crossword puzzle:

Down:

1. state that decided the election

3. office Bush was elected to in 2000 and 2004

4. Bush's opponent in 2000

Across:

2. Bush's political party

5. Bush's opponent in 2004

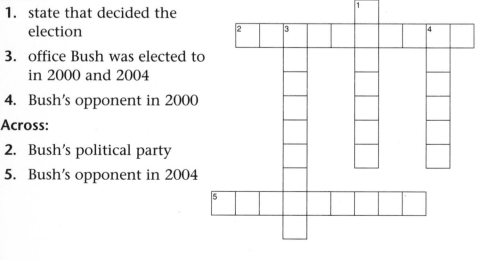

Presidential Survey

Think about and answer these questions. Answer each one with a different president.

1. Who is one of your favorite presidents?

   _____

   Why?

2. Name a president you would like to learn more about.

   _____

   Why?

   (Check your library for a biography of this president.)

3. Suppose you had a time machine. Which president would you like to meet in person? _____

   List one question you would ask.

4. Name a president you are not very interested in.

   _____

   Why not?

Birthplaces of Presidents by State

California

Richard M. Nixon

Nebraska

Gerald R. Ford

Texas

Dwight D Eisenhower

Lyndon B. Johnson

Iowa

Herbert Hoover

Missouri

Harry S. Truman

Arkansas

William Jefferson Clinton

Illinois

Ronald Reagan

Kentucky

Abraham Lincoln

Ohio

James A Garfield

Ulysses S. Grant

Warren G. Harding

Benjamin Harrison

Rutherford B. Hayes

William McKinley

William Howard Taft

New York

Millard Fillmore

Franklin D. Roosevelt

Theodore Roosevelt

Martin Van Buren

Vermont

Chester A. Arthur

Calvin Coolidge

New Hampshire

Franklin Pierce

Birthplaces of Presidents by State

Massachusetts
John Adams
John Quincy Adams
George Bush
John F. Kennedy

Connecticut
George W. Bush

New Jersey
Grover Cleveland

Pennsylvania
James Buchanan

Virginia
William Henry Harrison
Thomas Jefferson
James Madison
James Monroe
Zachary Taylor
John Tyler
George Washington
Woodrow Wilson

North Carolina
Andrew Johnson
James K. Polk

South Carolina
Andrew Jackson

Georgia
Jimmy Carter

69

Thinking about the Map

1. Why do you think more presidents were born on the eastern coast than any other place in the country?

   _____

2. Were any presidents born in the state where you were born or in the state where you now live?

   _____

   If so, name them. _____

   _____

3. Which state would you most like to visit and tour presidential birthplaces?

   _____

   Why? _____

4. Name one or two states you think will be the birthplace of many presidents in the future.

   _____

   Why? _____

   _____

5. How are the presidents born in Virginia and Ohio alike or different?

   _____

   _____

www.summerbridgeactivities.com   © Rainbow Bridge Publishing

Presidents Who Died in Office

Here is a list of the presidents who died in office. Those marked with an asterisk (*) were assassinated.

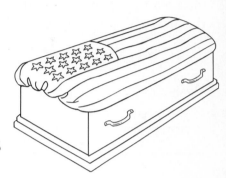

1. William Henry Harrison, 1841
2. Zachary Taylor, 1850
3. Abraham Lincoln, 1865*
4. James Garfield, 1881*
5. William McKinley, 1901*
6. Warren G. Harding, 1923
7. Franklin Delano Roosevelt, 1945
8. John F. Kennedy, 1963*

Thoughts to ponder:

1. Seven of these deaths happened in a regular pattern. Beginning with Harrison, the president elected every twenty years (1840, 1860, 1880, 1900, 1920, 1940, and 1960) died in office. The only exception was Zachary Taylor. Some people have called this a curse or a jinx. Others think it is simply a coincidence. In your dictionary, look up the words *curse*, *jinx*, and *coincidence*. Which do you think it is?

    _____

    _____

Why?

    _____

    _____

    _____

    _____

Presidents 4–5—RB-904000

Presidents Who Died in Office

2. Name a president whose death you think would have been particularly sad for the country.

_____

Why?

_____

_____

_____

3. Interview someone in your family or at your school who remembers the death of Franklin D. Roosevelt or John F. Kennedy. List details they remember.

_____

_____

_____

_____

4. The Secret Service is responsible for protecting the president. Name specific things you think the Secret Service should do to offer this protection.

_____

_____

_____

_____

_____

72

Compare and Contrast

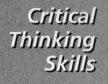

1. Name two presidents who were alike and tell how.

_____

_____

_____

_____

_____

2. Name two other presidents who were different and tell how.

_____

_____

_____

_____

_____

_____

3. List differences and similarities between two political parties (choose from Federalist, Democratic-Republican, Whig, Republican, and Democrat). Tell which you would belong to.

_____

_____

_____

_____

_____

_____

Presidential Autobiography

Pretend you are one of the presidents. Write your autobiography (the story of your life) in first person ("I did this" and "I did that"). You might answer such questions as the following: Was your family rich or poor? What did you like to do as a child? Whom did you marry? What were your great achievements? What were the problems you faced as president? Include as many details as possible.

_____

_____

_____

_____

_____

_____

_____

_____

_____

_____

_____

_____

_____

_____

_____

_____

_____

_____

_____

_____

_____

_____

www.summerbridgeactivities.com   © Rainbow Bridge Publishing

Presidential Autobiography

_____
_____
_____
_____
_____
_____
_____
_____
_____
_____
_____
_____
_____
_____
_____
_____
_____
_____
_____
_____
_____
_____
_____
_____
_____
_____
_____

Presidents 4–5—RB-904000

Answer Pages

Page 4
To begin with, initially, originally, in the beginning, from the start, highest priority, front

Page 6

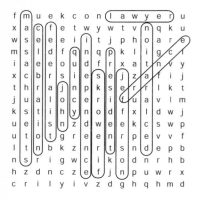

Jefferson, Declaration, Independence, president, lawyer, Massachusetts, France, John, Quincy, celebration, fireworks

Page 8
1. D   2. D
3. F   4. F
5. D   6. F

Page 10
1. A
2. A
3. B
4. A

Page 11
Missouri, Maine

Page 12
1. France
2. England
3. The Netherlands
4. Russia

Page 14
1. F   2. F
3. T   4. F
5. T

Page 16
1. B   2. C
3. B   4. D
5. A   6. A
7. C

Page 17
1. Clark
2. Lewis
3. 31
4. longer

Page 18
1. cardinal   2. Potomac
3. Richmond   4. dogwood
5. tobacco

Page 19
1. Nashville
2. Tennessee
3. Missouri, Kentucky, or Virginia
4. Mississippi, Alabama, or Georgia

Page 20

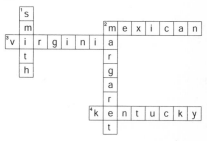

Answer Pages

Page 22
1. Hokkaido, Honshu, Shikoku, Kyushu
2. Kyushu
3. Honshu
4. Mt. Fuji

Page 23
1. Arizona, New Mexico
2. Texas
3. two
4. California

Page 24
1. Pennsylvania
2. minister to Russia, minister to Great Britain, or secretary of state
3. niece

Page 26
4
1
2
3
7
5
6

Page 28
1. South
2. Democratic
3. Eliza
4. Republicans
5. trial
6. Folly
7. Tennessee
   Secretary of War: STANTON

Page 30
1. B	2. A
3. B	4. A
5. Julia	6. 8
7. 9	8. 37

Page 31
1. Court
2. Finch
3. first
4. telephone
   State: OHIO

Page 32

appointment — naming someone for a job

reform — correcting something that is wrong

scandal — a dishonest act disgracing the people involved

merit — a good or valuable quality

wrongdoing — an immoral or illegal act

investigation — discovering information about something

Page 33
1. A
2. B
3. A
4. B

Page 35
Idioms

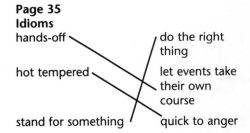

hands-off — let events take their own course

hot tempered — quick to anger

stand for something — do the right thing

Cause and Effect
1. C
2. C
3. C, E
4. C
5. E

77

Answer Pages

Page 36

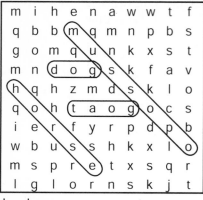

dog, horse, opossum, goat

Page 37
1. seventh, nine
2. twenty-fifth
3. first
4. fifth
5. eight
6. third

Page 39
able to do many things

Page 40
83 pounds

Page 42

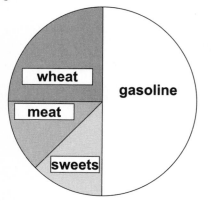

Page 43
1. 7,004,847
2. 7,000,000

Page 44
Answers will vary.

Page 46

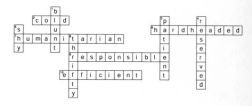

Page 48
1. Emergency Banking Act
2. Civilian Conservation Corps
3. Public Works Administration
4. Tennessee Valley Authority
5. Federal Deposit Insurance Corporation
6. Securities and Exchange Commission
7. Social Security

Page 50
1. He did not have trouble in school when he was young.
2. He did not play on the college football team.
3. The Truman Doctrine was not a program to help the poor.
4. The Korean War did not start before Truman became president.

Page 51
4
2
3
1

Answer Pages

Page 53

Jacqueline Kennedy

Lee Harvey Oswald

John Connally

Nellie Connally

Jack Ruby

Lyndon B. Johnson

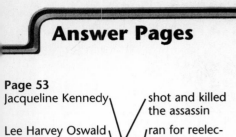

shot and killed the assassin

ran for reelection the year after JFK died

was in surgery when Kennedy died

became a widow at a young age

fired three shots with a rifle

spoke to JFK right before shots rang out

Page 61

1. Communicater   Communicator
2. Illnois   Illinois
3. acter   actor
4. apointed   appointed
5. moovies   movies

Page 62

1. raised
2. play
3. joined
4. started

Page 64

1. 2 years
2. 29 years older
3. 30 years after
4. Kennedy

Page 55

1. F
2. F
3. T
4. F
5. F
6. T
7. T

Page 57

E, C
C, E
E, C
C, E

Page 58

1. California
2. Illinois
3. Nebraska
4. Michigan

Page 59

1. F
2. F
3. T
4. T

Page 66

Page 67

Answers will vary.

Page 70

Answers will vary.

Page 71

Answers will vary.

Page 72

Answers will vary.

Page 73

Answers will vary.

Pages 74–75

Answers will vary.

Notes

Five things I'm
thankful for:

1. _____
2. _____
3. _____
4. _____
5. _____